More
Cooking With
OLD BAY ®

Great New Recipes
Featuring
Old Bay Seasoning

Acknowledgments

—Cover photograph by Burwell & Burwell, Washington, DC
—Design & Typesetting by Freudenheim Graves, Silver Spring, MD
—Cover graphics by Pearl and Associates, Inc., Boca Raton, FL
—Food styling by Robin Lutz

ISBN 0-942320-58-1

More... Quick Recipes for Creative Cooking!

The American Cooking Guild's *Collector's Series* includes over 30 popular cooking topics such as Barbeque, Breakfasts & Brunches, Chicken, Cookies, Hors d' Oeuvres, Seafood, Tea, Coffee, Pasta, Pizza, Salads, Italian and many more. Each book contains more than 50 selected recipes. For a catalog of these and many other full sized cookbooks, send $1 to the address below and a coupon will be included for $1 off your first order.

Cookbooks Make Great Premiums!

The American Cooking Guild has been the premier publisher of private label and custom cookbooks since 1981. Retailers, manufacturers, and food companies have all chosen The American Cooking Guild to publish their premium and promotional cookbooks. For further information on our special markets programs please contact the address below.

The American Cooking Guild

3600-K South Congress Avenue
Boynton Beach, FL 33426-8488

Contents

Celebrities Discover OLD BAY

OLD BAY Classics

Introduction

When we published the first OLD BAY® cookbook for our 50th anniversary, we were thrilled with the response. Who would have known that this cookbook would be an inspiration for people around the country, bringing back cherished memories about cooking with this unique seasoning. People wrote us, they phoned us and they filled us in on how OLD BAY Seasoning was their secret ingredient. They told us how the distinctive yellow and blue can became a staple seasoning in their cupboards. And they let us know how their passion for OLD BAY had resulted in their experimenting with it on everything from meats and chicken to vegetables and pizza.

That started us thinking! We began to look around the country for new twists to this old favorite. We realized that cooks everywhere had discovered unique ways to incorporate OLD BAY into their regional recipes.

This cookbook is a celebration of the best we found. It features winning recipes from home cooks and professional chefs. And, it goes beyond the expected—OLD BAY on seafood—offering ways to incorporate this seasoning on a host of other foods, from portobello mushrooms to chicken with raspberries. In fact, there's even an entire chapter on chicken recipes, developed by East Coast restaurant chefs. Plus, we feature some of the best ideas from Florida residents who entered our Florida recipe contest.

We've also included a section that features favorites from cookbook authors who have discovered this secret ingredient and made it an integral part of their cooking. And, of course, recipes of celebrities, born and raised in the Chesapeake Bay region, who grew up with this flavor and carried it with them to their new homes.

We haven't forgotten our heritage, however. **More Cooking with OLD BAY** wouldn't be complete if we didn't highlight specialties from our beloved Chesapeake Bay. We've included those OLD BAY favorites you've come to love, from steamed crabs and shrimp salad to a dynamic hot crab dip. We hope you'll add these recipes to your permanent collection, because we want to let you in on everyone's secret to great cooking.

Florida Discovers **OLD BAY**

With the flavor of OLD BAY® Seasoning spreading around the country, we began a regional recipe search in Florida, home to sumptuous seafood from the state's bounteous waters. We invited residents to send us their favorite OLD BAY recipes, and we were thrilled with some of the innovative ideas we found. Imagine swordfish, mango and OLD BAY! Or how about shrimp, pineapple and OLD BAY? Florida residents combine flavors that demonstrate the subtle way OLD BAY can complement and inspire unusual combinations.

Winners were selected from five Florida regions: Fort Myers/Naples, Jacksonville, Miami, Orlando and Tampa, and these winners were invited to participate in a cook-off in Tampa. In front of Florida food experts and a crowd of hungry Tampa residents, these Florida cooks grilled and sautéed for the state OLD BAY title.

Take some time to enjoy some of the diverse flavors we discovered. Enjoy the award-winning Salmon with Herb Sauce or the zesty Smoked Sausage Creole. We've also included some second- and third-place winners, including a Zippy Dipping Sauce for chicken and an easy stir-fry.

Salmon with Herb Sauce

This First Place Winner in the Florida cook-off received raves from the judges. A creamy herb sauce adds a special touch to fresh salmon fillets.

Cooking spray
1 ¼ pounds fresh salmon fillets
OLD BAY Seasoning

Coating Mix:

1 cup dried bread crumbs
1 tablespoon parsley flakes
1 tablespoon basil leaves
¼ teaspoon garlic powder
¼ cup unsalted butter
1 tablespoon fresh lime juice
1 tablespoon grated lime peel
1 teaspoon OLD BAY
  Seasoning

Herb Sauce:

⅓ cup heavy cream
⅓ cup sour cream
2 teaspoons dried chives
2 teaspoons basil leaves
1 teaspoon parsley flakes
Salt and pepper, to taste
1 tablespoon fresh lemon juice

Preheat oven to 400°.

Spray a large baking pan with cooking spray. Place the salmon on the baking sheet. Lightly sprinkle with OLD BAY.

In a medium bowl, combine the bread crumbs, parsley, basil and garlic.

In a large skillet over medium heat, melt the butter. Add the lime juice, lime peel, OLD BAY Seasoning and crumb mixture. Sauté the mixture over medium heat until crunchy, about 6 to 8 minutes.

Top each salmon fillet with some of the bread crumb mixture.

Bake the salmon at 400° for 15 minutes, or until done.

While the fish bakes, make the herb sauce. Combine the heavy cream, sour cream, chives, basil and parsley. Add salt and pepper, to taste. Stir in the lemon juice.

Serve the herb sauce with the fish.

Yield: 4 to 6 servings

Zita Wilensky, Miami, FL. 1st Place Cook-Off Winner

Pineapple Shrimp Pyramids

Winner of Florida's second prize, this imaginative shrimp recipe blends the sweetness of brown sugar with the tanginess of OLD BAY.

6 pieces aluminum foil, each 12 inches long
1 can (16 ounces) pineapple slices
1½ pounds raw medium shrimp, shelled and deveined
3 teaspoons OLD BAY Seasoning, divided
6 tablespoons finely chopped red bell pepper, divided
6 tablespoons brown sugar, divided
6 tablespoons butter, divided

Preheat oven to 350°.

Place one pineapple slice in the middle of each piece of aluminum foil. Arrange 6 to 8 shrimp on top of each pineapple slice and sprinkle with ½ teaspoon OLD BAY Seasoning.

Add 1 tablespoon red bell pepper and 1 tablespoon brown sugar to each serving. Top each serving with 1 tablespoon butter.

Bring the corners of the foil together up over the shrimp and twist to close, so that each packet resembles a large pyramid.

Place packets on a metal baking sheet and bake at 350° for about 20 minutes.

Yield: 6 servings

Capt. Charlie Williams, Fort Myers/Naples, FL. 2nd Place Cook-Off Winner

OLD BAY Crab Burritos

You can use canned or homemade chicken broth in this recipe. Top the burritos with shredded Swiss cheese, shredded lettuce, sour cream or chopped tomato.

10 flour tortillas
2 tablespoons vegetable oil
2 jalapeño peppers, minced
1 onion, thinly sliced
1 red bell pepper, thinly sliced
1 carrot, shredded
1 tablespoon OLD BAY Seasoning
½ teaspoon chili powder
1 cup cooked rice
1 cup chicken broth
1 pound crabmeat, shells removed
Shredded Swiss cheese, as a garnish
Shredded lettuce, as a garnish
Sour cream, as a garnish
Chopped tomato, as a garnish

Preheat oven to 300°.

Wrap the tortillas in aluminum foil and heat them in the oven while you prepare the crab filling.

Heat the oil in a large skillet over medium-high heat. Sauté the jalapeño peppers, onion, red bell pepper and carrot for 2 to 3 minutes, or just until crisp-tender.

Add the OLD BAY Seasoning, chili powder, rice and chicken broth. Simmer the vegetable mixture until most of the liquid is absorbed.

Gently stir in the crabmeat and heat through.

Remove the tortillas from the oven. Spoon some crab mixture onto each tortilla and roll it up. Garnish burritos with Swiss cheese, lettuce, sour cream and tomato.

Yield: 10 burritos

George M. Gallamore, Jr., Jacksonville, FL

Grilled Swordfish Loco with Fresh Mango Salsa

The mango salsa adds a fresh, tangy flavor to the grilled fish.

Marinade:

¼ cup olive oil
2 teaspoons OLD BAY Seasoning
¼ cup fresh lime juice
¼ cup tequila
1 teaspoon minced fresh cilantro
4 swordfish steaks, about 6 ounces each

Mango Salsa:

2 cups diced fresh mango
2 teaspoons orange zest
3 oranges, peeled, cored, chopped
½ cup sliced scallions
2 tablespoons chopped fresh cilantro
¾ teaspoons fresh ginger, grated
2 teaspoons jalapeño peppers, seeded and minced

To prepare the marinade: In a small bowl combine the olive oil, OLD BAY Seasoning, lime juice, tequila and cilantro. Place the marinade in a shallow glass dish or in a self-closing plastic bag. Place the swordfish steaks in the marinade, turning to coat. Let the steaks marinate for 20 to 30 minutes in the refrigerator.

To prepare the mango salsa: In a medium bowl, combine the mango, orange zest, oranges, onion, cilantro, ginger and jalapeño peppers.

Prepare the grill. Grill the marinated swordfish steaks over hot coals, using applewood or mesquite chips, for about 5 minutes per side or until done. Serve the grilled fish with the mango salsa.

Yield: 4 servings

George M. Heilman, Tampa, FL

Smoked Sausage Creole

This creole dish combines the rich flavors of onion, pepper and smoked sausage in a spicy broth.

2 tablespoons oil
1 medium onion, cut into 1-inch pieces
1 medium red or green bell pepper, cut into 1-inch pieces
1 pound smoked sausage, cut into ½-inch slices
1 large carrot, cut into ½-inch slices
1 tablespoon OLD BAY Seasoning
½ teaspoon garlic powder
⅛ teaspoon red pepper flakes, optional
1 bay leaf
4 cups chicken broth
3 tablespoons tomato paste
1½ cups orzo
1 can (14 ounces) black-eyed peas, drained
1 large zucchini, quartered and sliced

In a large Dutch oven or stock pot, heat the oil and sauté the onion and bell pepper for 2 to 3 minutes over medium-high heat.

Add the sausage and carrot and continue to cook until the sausage is browned, about 5 minutes.

Stir in the OLD BAY Seasoning, garlic, red pepper, bay leaf, chicken broth and tomato paste. Return to a boil, stirring frequently.

Add the orzo and black-eyed peas. Reduce heat to medium and simmer 3 minutes. Add the zucchini and cook another 7 minutes, until orzo is cooked through and zucchini is tender. Stir frequently.

Yield: 6 servings

Joy Petkov, Orlando, FL

Zippy Dipping Sauce

You'll find a million uses for this Zippy Dipping Sauce, so make a double batch.

¼ *cup honey*
2 tablespoons ketchup
1 teaspoon lemon juice
1 teaspoon OLD BAY Seasoning

In a small bowl, combine the honey, ketchup, lemon juice and OLD BAY Seasoning.
Yield: about ½ cup

Suggested uses:
- Use as a dipping sauce for broiled chicken
- Serve with steamed shrimp
- Brush on chicken during the last 10 minutes of baking or broiling
- Brush on fish during the last 10 minutes of baking
- Baste on pork roast

William Miller, Vero Beach, FL

Napa Shrimp Stir-Fry

Here is an untraditional stir-fry that goes together in just a few minutes.

2 tablespoons vegetable oil
2 cups shredded Napa cabbage
1 cup shredded jicama
1 cup shredded carrot
1 cup chopped green onion
1½ pounds medium shrimp, peeled and deveined
2 teaspoons OLD BAY Seasoning
½ cup chicken broth
2 tablespoons cornstarch
1 cup honey-roasted cashews
¼ cup chopped fresh parsley, as a garnish

In a wok or large skillet, heat the vegetable oil. Stir-fry the cabbage 2 minutes over medium-high heat.

Add the jicama, carrot, green onion, shrimp and OLD BAY Seasoning. Cook, stirring, for about 3 minutes.

In a small bowl, blend the chicken broth and cornstarch. Pour into the shrimp mixture and continue cooking until thickened. Stir frequently. Stir in the cashews and serve garnished with parsley.

Yield: 5 servings

Beverly Ann Crummey, Tampa, FL

Shrimp Apollo

This quickly assembled dish is perfect for busy nights when you want to eat well but get out of the kitchen in a hurry.

1 container (9 ounces) fresh pasta, any variety
1 tablespoon olive oil
¼ cup minced green onion
⅓ cup diced green bell pepper
1 package (8 ounces) cream cheese with olive and pimento
1 tablespoon OLD BAY Seasoning, divided
Milk, to thin the sauce
1 tablespoon lime juice
1 pound medium shrimp, peeled and deveined

Cook the pasta according to the package directions and keep warm.

Heat the olive oil in a large saucepan over medium heat. Add the green onion and green pepper and cook until tender, about 5 minutes. Turn the heat to low.

Add the cream cheese and ½ tablespoon OLD BAY Seasoning, stirring until smooth. Thin the sauce with a tablespoon or two of milk, if desired. Keep warm.

In a large saucepan, bring 1 quart water to a boil. Add ½ tablespoon OLD BAY Seasoning, lime juice and shrimp. Cook for 5 minutes or until the shrimp turn pink and are cooked through. Drain well.

To serve, ladle sauce over each serving of pasta and top with shrimp.

Yield: 4 servings

Lynn Newman, Jacksonville, FL

Bajan OLD BAY Trout

Bananas, rum and trout are combined in this unusual tropical trout dish.

2 teaspoons OLD BAY Seasoning
4 rainbow trout fillets, about 6 ounces each
1 cup all-purpose flour
½ cup unsalted butter
1 clove garlic, minced
½ cup dark rum
2 medium bananas, cut into ½-inch slices
¾ cup slivered almonds

Sprinkle the OLD BAY Seasoning over the trout fillets. Lightly dredge the fillets in flour.

Melt the butter in a large skillet over medium heat. Add the trout fillets and garlic to the melted butter. Sauté for about 6 minutes, turning once.

Remove the trout from the skillet and place on warmed dinner plates.

In the same skillet, add the rum, bananas and almonds. Cook for 1 minute, stirring constantly.

Top the fillets with the banana mixture. Serve immediately.
Yield: 4 servings

Nikki Peden, Orlando, FL

Shrimp-Stuffed Red Snapper

This is fancy enough for a dinner party and very quick to assemble. You can substitute other fish for the red snapper, if you prefer.

1 pound fresh red snapper fillets
2½ teaspoons OLD BAY Seasoning, divided
Vegetable cooking spray, for coating baking sheet
½ pound fresh shrimp, any size
1 small white onion, chopped
1 tablespoon butter or margarine
Provolone cheese, in thin slices
Lemon or lime wedges, as a garnish

Preheat oven to 400°.

Sprinkle the fish fillets with 1 teaspoon OLD BAY Seasoning. Place the fillets on a baking sheet sprayed with vegetable cooking spray.

Season the shrimp with 1 teaspoon OLD BAY Seasoning and place in a saucepan. Add ½ cup water and bring to a boil. Cover and let boil for 5 minutes. Peel, devein and finely chop the shrimp.

Sauté the onion in the butter until tender. Add the shrimp and remaining ½ teaspoon OLD BAY Seasoning.

Bake the fillets in a 400° oven for 10 to 12 minutes. Remove the fish from the oven and place an equal amount of shrimp stuffing mixture in the center of each fillet. Top each fillet with 1 slice of provolone cheese.

Preheat broiler and broil until the cheese melts, about 1 minute. Garnish each fillet with OLD BAY Seasoning and a wedge of lemon or lime.

Yield: 4 servings

Jane Podowski, Miami, FL

Grilled Caribbean Tuna with Black Bean Mango Salsa

Black beans and mangoes provide an unusual twist to this salsa. Easy to prepare, this recipe is perfect for entertaining.

Salsa:

1 can (14½ ounces) black beans, drained
1¼ cups peeled and diced mango
1 red onion, peeled and diced
1 jalapeño pepper, seeded and finely diced
½ cup chopped fresh cilantro
½ cup lime juice
¼ cup olive oil
1 teaspoon OLD BAY Seasoning
Salt and pepper, to taste

Tuna:

½ cup olive oil
1 tablespoon OLD BAY Seasoning
4 fresh tuna steaks, each 8 ounces and ½-inch thick
12 Belgian endive leaves, as a garnish
4 fresh basil sprigs, as a garnish

To prepare the salsa: In a medium bowl, combine all salsa ingredients. Mix well and set aside.

To prepare the tuna: In a small bowl, combine olive oil and OLD BAY Seasoning.

Brush the seasoned oil on both sides of the tuna fillets. Place the tuna on a prepared grill and cook over medium-hot coals, about 5 minutes per side. Halfway through cooking, brush the tuna again with the seasoned oil.

To serve, place the grilled tuna on a bed of salsa. Garnish each serving with 3 endive leaves and a sprig of basil.

Yield: 4 servings

Diana M. Hanau, Miami, FL

Cooking with Pride

In recent years, hometown OLD BAY® fans have begun experimenting with this traditional seafood seasoning on everything from french fries to chicken. Understanding the versatility of this flavor, OLD BAY asked the professionals—restaurant chefs along the East Coast—for their most creative recipes using OLD BAY on chicken.

OLD BAY Seasoning partnered with Pride of Baltimore II, the only existing replica of an 1812-era Baltimore Clipper topsail schooner. During Pride II's Chesapeake Bay and East Coast Tour, OLD BAY traveled to Baltimore, Boston, New York, Norfolk, Philadelphia and Washington, DC to host the OLD BAY Neighborhood Challenge.

In each port, OLD BAY invited restaurants throughout the city to create their favorite chicken dish using OLD BAY. At each event, a distinguished panel of food journalists selected the winner of the Critic's Choice award. In addition, the public tasted and rated these recipes to determine the recipient of the People's Choice honor.

The Critic's Choice and People's Choice recipes from each city are featured in this section, along with some of our personal favorites.

Potato and Chicken Latkes

JW's Steakhouse at the Philadelphia Marriott created this first place winner. An unusual twist to the traditional potato latke.

Relish:

¼ cup butter
½ cup diced andouille sausage
1½ cups frozen white corn
6 plum tomatoes, chopped
1 green bell pepper, chopped
2 tablespoons brown sugar
½ teaspoon cracked black
   pepper
½ teaspoon salt
Cornstarch and water, optional

Latkes:

½ cup boneless chicken breasts,
   cooked, shredded by hand
2 cups shredded potatoes, fresh
   or frozen
1 green onion, chopped
1 egg yolk
2 teaspoons OLD BAY
   Seasoning
2 cloves garlic, minced
½ teaspoon ground black
   pepper
½ teaspoon salt
2 tablespoons butter
Sour cream, as a garnish

To make the relish: In a medium skillet, melt butter on medium-high heat. Add the relish ingredients and sauté for 20 minutes. Add cornstarch and water to thicken, if desired.

To make the latkes: In a large bowl, combine the chicken, potatoes, green onion, egg yolk, OLD BAY Seasoning, garlic, black pepper and salt. Set aside.

Melt butter on medium-high heat in a non-stick skillet. Shape the latke mixture into small individual patties or spread the mixture in the skillet into one large pancake shape. Cook the latkes on low to medium heat until nicely browned on both sides.

Place one-fourth of the relish in the center of four serving plates. Arrange slices or individual pieces of latke on top of the relish.

Serve with sour cream, if desired.

Yield: 4 servings

OLD BAY Rum Runner Chicken

During OLD BAY's trip with the Pride II, the company landed at South Street Seaport in New York. This recipe was developed by the Liberty Cafe and Oyster Bar, Pier 17 Pavilion. The boiled potatoes are great for soaking up the flavorful sauce.

1 tablespoon cornstarch
1 tablespoon OLD BAY Seasoning
½ cup chicken broth
¼ cup dark rum
2 tablespoons dark brown sugar
¼ teaspoon allspice
1 pound boneless, skinless chicken breasts, cut in strips
½ teaspoon OLD BAY Seasoning
1 tablespoon oil

1 cup chopped celery
1 small green bell pepper, cut in thin strips
1 small red bell pepper, cut in thin strips
2 jalapeño peppers, finely chopped
1 small onion, cut in thin strips
4 boiled potatoes, sliced
Shredded coconut, as a garnish

In a small bowl, blend the cornstarch, 1 tablespoon OLD BAY Seasoning and the chicken broth. Set aside.

In a separate bowl, mix the rum, brown sugar and allspice. Set aside.

Season the chicken strips with ½ teaspoon OLD BAY Seasoning.

In a skillet, heat the oil over medium heat. Sauté the chicken 3 to 5 minutes or until done. Remove the chicken from the pan and keep warm.

To the same skillet, add the celery, green bell pepper, red bell pepper, jalapeño peppers and onion. Sauté 2 to 3 minutes. Return the chicken to the skillet. Stir in the rum mixture and bring to a boil. Pour in the cornstarch-broth mixture. Stir until the sauce is slightly thickened.

Serve the chicken over boiled potatoes and sprinkle each serving with a little shredded coconut.

Yield: 4 to 6 servings

Chicken and Shrimp in Sherry Cream Sauce

This velvety cream sauce won accolades for Blue Pete's Restaurant, a favorite dining spot of visitors to Virginia Beach.

½ pound boneless, skinless chicken breasts, cut into strips
1 tablespoon all-purpose flour
3 tablespoons butter
¼ pound mushrooms, thinly sliced
¼ cup finely chopped shallots
1 teaspoon OLD BAY Seasoning
½ pound shrimp, peeled and deveined
½ cup dry sherry
½ cup heavy cream
1 pound any pasta, cooked and drained

Coat the chicken strips lightly with flour. In a skillet, melt the butter over medium-high heat. Add the chicken and sauté for 2 to 3 minutes.

Add the mushrooms and shallots. Stir in the OLD BAY Seasoning. Cook 5 minutes.

Add the shrimp and cook another 3 to 5 minutes or until the shrimp turn pink.

Stir the sherry into the pan and simmer for about 3 to 5 minutes. Add the heavy cream and stir constantly until the sauce thickens.

Serve over pasta of your choice.

Yield: 4 servings

Café 21 Stuffed Chicken Breasts

Café 21 in downtown Norfolk created this People's Choice and Critic's Choice winner.When preparing, don't forget the sauce. It's a surefire hit.

4 boneless, skinless chicken breast halves

Stuffing:

2 tablespoons olive oil
½ cup finely chopped red onion
½ cup finely chopped celery
½ pound crabmeat, optional
2 teaspoons OLD BAY Seasoning, for stuffing

Coating:

1 cup plain bread crumbs
1 teaspoon basil leaves
1 tablespoon fresh chopped parsley
1 teaspoon OLD BAY Seasoning, for bread crumbs
¼ cup OLD BAY Seasoning, for dredging
1 egg, slightly beaten
¼ cup olive oil

Sauce:

1 cup orange marmalade
3 tablespoons Dijon mustard
¾ cup white wine

To prepare the chicken: Using a sharp knife, cut a deep slit into the side of each chicken breast to form a pocket. Set aside.

In a skillet, heat 2 tablespoons olive oil over medium-high heat. Sauté the onion and celery until tender.

Add crabmeat, if desired, and 2 teaspoons OLD BAY Seasoning. Stir until warmed through. Set aside.

In a small bowl, combine bread crumbs, basil, parsley and 1 teaspoon OLD BAY Seasoning. Set aside.

Stuff each chicken breast with the stuffing mixture. Fasten with a toothpick, if necessary. Dredge the stuffed breasts in ¼ cup OLD BAY Seasoning. Dip in the beaten egg, then in the bread crumb mixture. Heat ¼ cup olive oil over medium-high heat.

Sauté the chicken breasts in the olive oil for 5 to 7 minutes per side, or until done.

To make the sauce: In a saucepan over medium heat, combine the orange marmalade, Dijon mustard and white wine. Reduce until slightly thickened.

Remove the toothpicks from the chicken breasts and spoon the sauce over the chicken just before serving.

Yield: 4 servings

Creole Chicken and Shrimp Gumbo

Critics loved this recipe from Southside 815 in Alexandria, VA. It makes a hearty meal for a cold winter night.

1 tablespoon olive oil
1 pound boneless, skinless chicken breasts, cut in cubes
½ cup diced andouille sausage
1 cup sliced okra
1 cup chopped green bell pepper
1 cup chopped red bell pepper
1 cup chopped onion
½ cup chopped celery
½ pound large shrimp, peeled and deveined
1 tablespoon OLD BAY Seasoning
½ teaspoon thyme leaves
2 cups low-sodium chicken broth
2 cups tomato juice
½ cup tomato paste
Lemon wedges and fresh parsley, as a garnish
Cooked rice

In a Dutch oven or large saucepan, heat the olive oil over medium-high heat. Sauté the chicken cubes for 3 to 5 minutes. Add the sausage and chopped vegetables. Cook for 2 to 3 minutes.

Add the shrimp, OLD BAY Seasoning and thyme. Cook for 2 to 3 minutes. Add the chicken broth, tomato juice and tomato paste. Bring to a boil and simmer for 8 to 10 minutes. Remove from heat.

Serve over cooked rice. Garnish with lemon wedges and sprigs of parsley.

Yield: 4 to 6 servings

Crispy Jalapeño Honey Chicken

Enjoy this Washington, DC Critics Choice winner from the Park Promenade Hyatt Regency. A wonderful combination of diverse flavors that complement one another makes this chicken a star.

Chicken:

1½ cups unseasoned dry bread crumbs
1 teaspoon parsley flakes
3 tablespoons OLD BAY Seasoning, divided
¾ cup all-purpose flour
2 tablespoons honey
1 teaspoon finely chopped jalapeño pepper
1 clove garlic, minced
1 egg, beaten with 1 tablespoon water
4 boneless, skinless chicken breast halves
¼ cup vegetable oil

Tomato Relish:

1 tablespoon butter
2 tablespoons lemon juice
2 plum tomatoes, chopped
1 clove garlic, minced
⅛ teaspoon cracked black pepper

To prepare the chicken: On a plate, mix the bread crumbs and parsley with 2 tablespoons OLD BAY Seasoning.

On a separate plate, mix the flour and 1 tablespoon OLD BAY Seasoning.

In a shallow bowl, blend the honey, jalapeño pepper and garlic.

Coat the chicken breasts with the honey mixture. Dredge the chicken in the flour mixture, dip in the egg wash and roll in the bread crumb mixture.

In a skillet, heat the vegetable oil over medium-high heat. Sauté the chicken until golden brown on both sides, or until no longer pink. Set aside and keep warm.

To make the relish: In a small skillet, melt the butter over medium heat. Add the lemon juice, plum tomatoes, garlic and black pepper. Sauté for 3 to 5 minutes. Serve the chicken topped with the relish.

Yield: 4 servings

Waterman's Chicken

Created by Sam & Harry's, one of Washington DC's most prestigious restaurants, this chicken blends some of the freshest vegetables to make a flavorful stuffing.

Stuffing:

2 cups yellow whole kernel corn, fresh or frozen
2 eggs
½ pound crabmeat, all shell removed
½ cup finely chopped green bell pepper
½ cup finely chopped red bell pepper
½ cup finely chopped onion

Chicken:

4 boneless, skinless chicken breasts
2 tablespoons OLD BAY Seasoning
½ cup cornmeal
2 teaspoons cornstarch
2 tablespoons olive oil

Sauce:

2 ripe tomatoes, chopped
½ cup finely chopped red bell pepper
½ cup finely chopped green bell pepper
1 tablespoon dried cilantro
½ teaspoon minced garlic
½ teaspoon ground cumin
½ teaspoon OLD BAY Seasoning
½ cup low-sodium chicken broth
3 tablespoons white wine

To make the stuffing: Puree the corn in a blender or food processor until smooth. Add the eggs and process until mixed. Empty into a bowl and fold in the crabmeat, green pepper, red pepper and onion.

To make the chicken: Cut a deep slit into the side of each chicken breast to form a pocket, without going all the way through. Sprinkle OLD BAY Seasoning inside of each pocket.

Stuff each chicken breast with filling. Seal with toothpicks.

Sprinkle each stuffed breast with OLD BAY Seasoning.

In a small bowl, mix the cornmeal and cornstarch. Carefully coat each stuffed chicken breast.

In a skillet, heat the olive oil over medium-high heat. Sauté the chicken 3 to 5 minutes per side. Remove the chicken from pan and keep warm.

To make the sauce: In the same skillet over medium-high heat, sauté the tomatoes, red pepper and green pepper for 2 to 3 minutes. Stir in the cilantro, garlic, cumin, ½ teaspoon OLD BAY Seasoning, chicken broth and white wine. Add the chicken to the mixture and bring to a boil. Cover and simmer 15 to 20 minutes, turning the chicken once. Carefully remove the toothpicks from the chicken and serve with rice and black beans.

Yield: 4 servings

OLD BAY Citrus Chicken

Raspberries and field greens make this colorful entree perfect for a spring dinner. Berry and Elliot's at the Hyatt Regency City Hotel in Baltimore created a citrus vinaigrette that complements the chicken.

Vinaigrette:

¾ cup orange juice
½ cup honey
¼ cup lime juice
1 shallot, chopped
1½ tablespoons Dijon mustard
2 teaspoons chopped chives
2 teaspoons OLD BAY Seasoning
2 teaspoons balsamic vinegar
½ teaspoon salt

Chicken:

½ cup all-purpose flour
½ cup cornmeal

1 tablespoon OLD BAY Seasoning
2 teaspoons lemon pepper seasoning
2 teaspoons oregano
4 boneless, skinless chicken breast halves
2 tablespoons olive oil
2 cups tender mixed field greens
Fresh snipped chives, as a garnish
Fresh or frozen raspberries, as a garnish
Orange segments, as a garnish

To make the vinaigrette: In a medium bowl, whisk together the orange juice, honey, lime juice, shallot, Dijon mustard, chives, OLD BAY Seasoning, balsamic vinegar and salt. Set aside.

To prepare the chicken: On a shallow plate, mix the flour, cornmeal, OLD BAY Seasoning, lemon pepper seasoning and oregano. Dredge the chicken breasts in the flour mixture.

In a skillet over medium-high heat, heat the olive oil and sauté the chicken breasts for 7 to 10 minutes per side. Place the chicken on individual serving plates.

Toss the mixed field greens with enough vinaigrette to coat. Top each chicken breast with the greens. Drizzle with vinaigrette. Garnish with chives, raspberries and orange segments.

Yield: 4 servings

Seared Young Breast of Chicken

An Asian vegetable relish and fresh apricot tomato chutney highlight this winner from the Pavilion Restaurant at the Walters Art Gallery in Baltimore. Substitute dried apricots for fresh ones if they are not in season.

Chutney:

2 whole tomatoes, chopped
2 whole shallots, chopped
2 cups chopped fresh apricots or peaches
1 cup vinegar
½ cup water
¼ cup brown sugar
¼ cup OLD BAY Seasoning
2½ teaspoons curry powder

Vegetable Relish:

1 cup bean sprouts
½ cup red bell pepper, julienne
½ cup yellow bell pepper, julienne
½ cup bok choy, julienne
4 green onions, julienne
¼ lb. angel hair pasta, cooked, drained and chilled

Vinaigrette:

½ cup vegetable oil
¼ cup lemon juice
¼ cup honey
2 tablespoons finely chopped ginger
3 cloves garlic, minced

Chicken:

1 teaspoon ground allspice
4 boneless, skinless chicken breast halves
1 tablespoon vegetable oil

To make the chutney: In a medium non-reactive saucepan, combine the chutney ingredients. Bring to a boil and simmer for 45 to 50 minutes.

To prepare the vegetable relish: In a large bowl, mix together the bean sprouts and julienne vegetables. Add the chilled pasta.

To prepare the vinaigrette: In a small bowl, blend the vinaigrette ingredients. Pour over the vegetables and pasta. Toss to combine.

To cook the chicken: Rub the allspice into the chicken breasts and let stand for 5 minutes. Heat 1 tablespoon vegetable oil in a medium skillet. Sauté the chicken breasts over medium heat for 7 to 10 minutes per side.

To serve, place the chicken breasts on a bed of vegetable relish. Top with chutney.

Yield: 4 servings

Pollo Della Baia di Baltimore

A wonderful salad topped with chicken breast comes from Germano's Trattoria Petrucci in Little Italy, Baltimore.

Marinade:

½ cup olive oil
¼ cup balsamic vinegar
1 tablespoon OLD BAY Seasoning
1 teaspoon basil leaves
1 teaspoon rosemary leaves
4 boneless, skinless chicken breasts

Salad:

½ cup olive oil
¼ cup balsamic vinegar
1 teaspoon Dijon mustard
4 cups tender mixed salad greens
3 scallions, sliced thin
1 cucumber, sliced thin
1 carrot, sliced thin

To prepare the chicken: In a glass dish, blend together marinade ingredients. Add the chicken breasts and stir to coat. Marinate for 15 to 20 minutes. Remove the chicken from the marinade.

In a skillet, sauté the chicken breasts over medium heat for 5 to 6 minutes per side or until done.

To make the salad: In a small bowl, blend remaining olive oil, balsamic vinegar and Dijon mustard. Set aside.

In a bowl, combine the mixed salad greens, scallions, cucumber and carrot. Toss the salad with the vinaigrette just before serving. Serve the salad topped with the chicken breasts.

Yield: 4 servings

The Rusty Scupper's Pasta

The Rusty Scupper in Baltimore's Inner Harbor showcased this recipe in the Challenge. It's great when you are in a hurry and want something quick and delicious.

Seasoned Flour:

¼ cup all-purpose flour
1 tablespoon OLD BAY Seasoning
1½ teaspoons salt
1¼ teaspoons white pepper
1 teaspoon onion powder

Chicken and Shrimp Pasta:

1 pound boneless, skinless chicken breasts, cut in ½-inch strips
2 tablespoons butter
½ pound shrimp, peeled and deveined
½ teaspoon salt
½ cup heavy cream
2 cups pasta, cooked and drained
2 green onions, sliced

In a small bowl, combine all ingredients for the seasoned flour.

Coat the chicken strips with the seasoned flour mixture.

In a skillet, melt the butter over medium heat. Sauté the chicken strips for 2 to 3 minutes. Add the shrimp and sauté until the shrimp turn pink. Stir in the salt and heavy cream. Cook until the sauce thickens.

Add the cooked pasta and green onions and cook until heated through.

Yield: 5 servings

Pan-Seared Chicken Breast

Fresh salsa and citrus butter are great complements to this dish from Top of the Hub, in Boston.

Salsa:

¼ cup lime juice
¼ cup olive oil
¼ cup chopped fresh cilantro
5 green onions, chopped
2 tomatoes, seeded and chopped
1 jalapeño pepper, finely chopped

Chicken:

4 boneless, skinless chicken breast halves
2 teaspoons OLD BAY Seasoning
½ cup all-purpose flour
2 tablespoons olive oil

Citrus Butter:

½ cup butter
4 tablespoons frozen orange juice concentrate
1 cup heavy cream

¼ cup lime juice, optional

To make the salsa: In a medium bowl, combine the lime juice, olive oil, cilantro, green onions, tomatoes and jalapeño pepper. Set aside.

To make the chicken: Sprinkle the chicken breast halves with OLD BAY Seasoning. Dredge the chicken in flour.

In a skillet, heat 2 tablespoons olive oil over medium-high heat. Sauté the chicken breasts for 7 to 10 minutes per side.

To prepare the citrus butter: In a saucepan, melt the butter over medium heat. Stir in the orange juice and heavy cream. Cook over low heat 2 to 3 minutes. Season with lime juice, if desired.

Spoon a small amount of citrus butter onto each individual serving plate. Place the chicken breast in the center and top with the salsa.

Yield: 4 servings

Pistachio Chicken with Mixed Greens

Pistachios make a crunchy coating for this chicken, created by Cafe Marliave in Boston. If you like spice, add a little extra OLD BAY into the coating.

Dressing:

½ cup olive oil
¼ cup vinegar
¼ cup water
¼ cup grated Parmesan cheese
1 tablespoon sour cream
1 tablespoon lemon juice
1 clove garlic, minced
2 teaspoons OLD BAY Seasoning
1½ teaspoons dried minced onion
Mixed salad greens
Croutons, as a garnish
Whole pistachio nuts, as a garnish
Orange sections, as a garnish

Chicken:

8 ounces pistachio nuts, finely chopped
1 tablespoon OLD BAY Seasoning
1 pound boneless, skinless chicken breasts,
    pounded to ¼-inch thickness
½ cup all-purpose flour
1 egg, beaten with 1 tablespoon water
¼ cup oil

To prepare the dressing: In a small bowl, combine olive oil, vinegar, water, Parmesan cheese, sour cream, lemon juice, garlic, OLD BAY Seasoning and onion. Whisk. Set aside.

To make the chicken: Combine the chopped pistachio nuts with 1 tablespoon OLD BAY Seasoning. Set aside. Coat the flattened chicken breasts with flour. Shake off the excess. Dip the chicken into the egg wash. Coat each piece of chicken in the pistachio coating.

In a skillet, heat ¼ cup olive oil over medium heat. Sauté the chicken breasts for 8 to 10 minutes per side, or until done.

To serve, coat the mixed salad greens with the desired amount of dressing. Place the salad on individual serving plates and arrange the chicken on top of the greens (the chicken may be left whole or thinly sliced). Garnish with croutons, whole pistachio nuts and orange sections.

Yield: 4 servings

Celebrities Discover **OLD BAY**

Celebrities Discover **OLD BAY**

In recent years, we've noticed that everyone is discovering our secret ingredient. Throughout our wanderings, we've seen renowned cookbook authors incorporate OLD BAY® in numerous recipes. Celebrities from Maryland who discovered the taste while growing up add OLD BAY to their favorite foods. And, restaurants from across the country experiment with flavors that feature OLD BAY.

We talked to celebrities—we spoke to cookbook authors. We asked them for their favorite OLD BAY recipes. We found some fabulous crab cakes—and some unusual combinations such as an intensely-flavored middle eastern marinade for char-grilled skirt steak.

The next pages feature some of the best ideas we discovered. We hope you enjoy eating them as much as we did.

Kareem Abdul-Jabbar's
Catfish

This favorite from the famed basketball star is served at Georgia, the popular Los Angeles restaurant in which Abdul-Jabbar has an interest.

Fish:
3 pounds catfish
1 tablespoon salt
1 tablespoon cayenne pepper
1 tablespoon paprika
2 teaspoons garlic powder
1 tablespoon onion powder
2 teaspoons black pepper
1 teaspoon dried thyme
Vegetable oil, for deep frying

Breading:
1 cup cornmeal
2 tablespoons OLD BAY
  Seasoning
1 tablespoon onion powder
1 tablespoon garlic powder
¼ teaspoon cayenne pepper
¼ teaspoon black pepper

Pat the catfish fillets or nuggets with paper towels to dry them off.

In a large, flat dish, combine the salt, cayenne pepper, paprika, garlic, onion powder, 2 teaspoons black pepper and thyme. Coat the catfish with the seasoning mixture. Cover the catfish with plastic wrap and refrigerate overnight.

To prepare the breading, combine the cornmeal, OLD BAY Seasoning, onion powder, garlic, cayenne pepper and black pepper in bowl. Dip the seasoned catfish into the breading mixture to coat evenly.

In a deep skillet, heat the vegetable oil to a temperature of 365°. When the oil is hot, add the fish a few pieces at a time and deep-fry on both sides until golden brown, about 7 to 10 minutes. Drain on paper towels.

Yield: 6 servings

Barbara Smith's
Pan-Fried Crab Cakes with Chili Mayonnaise

These extraordinary crab cakes are among the more popular entrees at B. Smith's restaurants in Manhattan's Theater District and Washington's Union Station.

Chili Mayonnaise:

1 cup mayonnaise
2 tablespoons jalapeño pepper, minced
Hot pepper sauce, to taste

Crab Cakes:

1 tablespoon unsalted butter
½ cup finely chopped onion
½ cup finely chopped celery
1 pound fresh crabmeat
¾ cup unseasoned dried bread crumbs, divided
1 large egg
1 tablespoon mayonnaise
1 tablespoon sour cream
1 teaspoon chopped fresh dill
1 teaspoon OLD BAY Seasoning
½ teaspoon garlic powder
2 tablespoons vegetable oil

To make the chili mayonnaise: In a small bowl, combine mayonnaise, jalapeño pepper and hot pepper sauce. Cover and chill until needed.

To make the crab cakes: In a small skillet, melt the butter. Sauté the onion and celery until soft. Set aside.

In a large mixing bowl, stir together the crabmeat, ¼ cup bread crumbs, the reserved onion-celery mixture, egg, mayonnaise, sour cream, dill, OLD BAY Seasoning and garlic. Gently mix to combine.

Using damp hands, gently mold the mixture into 1-inch appetizer or 4-inch entrée patties.

Coat each crab cake with remaining bread crumbs.

In a large skillet, heat the vegetable oil. Fry the crab cakes on both sides for 4 to 6 minutes, or until golden brown. Serve with chili mayonnaise.

Yield: 8 appetizer servings or 4 entrée servings

Terresse Harding's
OLD BAY Vinaigrette

This much-requested recipe was created by Terresse Harding, co-executive chef of The Classic Catering People and is a featured recipe of Classic Catering of Baltimore.

1 cup olive oil
½ cup rice wine vinegar
3 tablespoons OLD BAY Seasoning
3 tablespoons lemon juice
2 tablespoons fresh chopped dill
½ teaspoon grated lemon rind

In small bowl, whisk together the olive oil, rice wine vinegar, OLD BAY Seasoning, lemon juice, dill and lemon rind.

Serve over mixed salad.

Yield: about 1½ cups

Jane Buffum's
Mushrooms Florentine

Portobello mushrooms are great as a main course because of their meaty taste. This recipe was created by food journalist and culinary consultant Jane Buffum.

4 portobello mushrooms (3 to 4 inches in diameter)
1 tablespoon olive oil
1 teaspoon OLD BAY Seasoning, divided
1 package (9 ounces) frozen creamed spinach, thawed
1 cup (4 ounces) grated Cheddar cheese
Strips of pimento or roasted pepper, as a garnish

Remove stems from the mushrooms. Clean the mushrooms with a soft brush.

Brush the mushrooms lightly with the olive oil. Sprinkle each mushroom with ¼ teaspoon OLD BAY Seasoning.

Place on a broiler pan with cap side up. Broil, 6 to 8 inches from heat, 8 to 10 minutes or until brown.

Turn the mushrooms over. Fill each with ¼ of the thawed spinach. Sprinkle with Cheddar cheese. Garnish with several strips of pimento or roasted pepper, if desired. Broil until the cheese is melted. Serve as a main course or as a side dish.

Note: This recipe can be modified as an appetizer by substituting 24 white button mushrooms for the portobellos and dividing the ingredients equally. Reduce cooking time accordingly.

Michael Tucker's
Maryland Crab Cakes

This recipe was created by actor Michael Tucker, a former Baltimorean. It appeared in *Baltimore* magazine in June 1995. Michael warns fellow cooks to use a white bread soft enough to disappear without a trace!

1 egg
2 tablespoons mayonnaise
3 slices soft white bread, crusts removed, cut in ½-inch chunks
Dash Worcestershire sauce
1 heaping teaspoon honey mustard
OLD BAY Seasoning, to taste
1 pound fresh crabmeat, well picked over
Peanut oil, for frying
Lard, for frying

In a small bowl, combine the egg, mayonnaise, white bread, Worcestershire sauce, honey mustard and OLD BAY Seasoning, to taste.

Place the picked crabmeat in a large bowl and pour the egg mixture over the top. Mix and let stand for about 20 minutes.

Using damp hands, gently form the crabmeat mixture into 4 ball-shaped cakes.

Heat a large cast-iron skillet with a mixture of peanut oil and lard, about 1 inch deep, to 350°. Fry the crab cakes until golden brown. Drain on paper towels.

Serve with honey mustard, cocktail sauce or tartar sauce.

Yield: 4 servings

Michael Chmar's
Tortilla Soup

Michael Chmar, who is the sous-chef at the famous Star Canyon in Dallas, created this glorious soup. He was formerly a chef at Baltimore's Milton Inn. Make a batch and serve when company comes over.

1 tablespoon olive oil
1 onion, chopped
1 carrot, chopped
5 garlic cloves, chopped
1 cup white wine
1 jar (12 ounces) sweet roasted red peppers or
  2 fresh roasted red bell peppers, peeled and seeded
3 plum tomatoes, chopped
1 can (4 ounces) chopped green chiles
1 bay leaf
6 cups chicken broth
5 corn tortillas, fried or toasted crisp
3 tablespoons fresh cilantro leaves, chopped
1 tablespoon OLD BAY Seasoning
1 teaspoon ground cumin
¾ teaspoon basil leaves
½ teaspoon thyme leaves
Fried tortilla strips, as a garnish
Sour cream, as a garnish
Fresh cilantro sprigs, as a garnish

Heat the olive oil in a large saucepan over medium-high heat. Add the onion, carrot and garlic. Sauté 5 minutes or until the onion is transparent.

Add the white wine, red peppers, tomatoes, chiles, bay leaf and chicken broth. Bring to a boil. Cover and simmer 30 minutes.

Break the tortillas into small pieces and add to the soup. Add the remaining ingredients. Simmer 10 minutes. Remove from heat.

In several small batches, transfer the soup to a blender or food processor. Purée 3 minutes or until smooth. If desired, strain the soup through a medium sieve to remove any excess seeds. Ladle the soup into bowls and garnish each serving with tortilla strips, sour cream and a sprig of cilantro.

Yield: Makes 8 servings

Note: Red chiles can be substituted for the green chiles, if desired.

OLD BAY TIP OF THE DAY

Herb Rub for Roasted Chicken or Turkey: Preheat oven to 375°. Rinse a whole chicken or turkey breast and pat dry. Combine 1 tablespoon OLD BAY Seasoning with 1½ teaspoons thyme and 1½ teaspoons rosemary. Rub the spice mixture over the whole chicken or turkey breast. Bake for 60 to 90 minutes, or until the internal temperature of the poultry reaches 185°. Yield: 8 servings

Perla Meyers'
Spicy Corn, Shrimp and Red Pepper Salad

Award-winning cookbook author Perla Meyers combines fresh summer vegetables with shrimp and OLD BAY in this recipe from her newest cookbook.

4 cups water
1 teaspoon OLD BAY Seasoning
½ pound medium shrimp
5 tablespoons extra-virgin olive oil, divided
2 tablespoons sherry vinegar, divided
2 large garlic cloves, peeled and mashed
Salt and freshly ground black pepper, to taste
Juice of 1 lime
1 small red onion, peeled and finely minced
1-2 teaspoons finely minced jalapeño pepper
1 large red bell pepper, cored, seeded and finely diced
4 cups cooked fresh corn kernels
3 tablespoons fresh cilantro leaves
Pinch cayenne pepper
Sprigs of fresh cilantro, as a garnish
Ripe cherry tomatoes, halved, as a garnish

In a saucepan, combine the water and OLD BAY Seasoning. Simmer for 1 minute, add the shrimp and poach until the shrimp just turn pink, about 1 to 2 minutes. Do not overcook. Drain well. Peel and cube the shrimp and set aside.

In a small bowl, combine 2 tablespoons olive oil, 1 tablespoon sherry vinegar and 1 mashed garlic clove and whisk until well blended. Add the shrimp and season with salt and pepper. Refrigerate for 30 minutes.

Combine remaining olive oil, sherry vinegar and garlic together with the lime juice, red onion and jalapeño pepper and whisk until well blended. Add the shrimp, red bell pepper, corn and cilantro. Season with salt and pepper and a pinch of cayenne pepper and toss well. Cover and chill for 2 hours.

To serve, bring the salad back to room temperature. Correct the seasoning and garnish with sprigs of cilantro and cherry tomatoes.

Yield: 6 servings

OLD BAY TIP OF THE DAY

Herb Poultry Stuffing: Sauté 2 tablespoons chopped onion in ½ cup butter until tender. Stir in 1 ½ teaspoons OLD BAY Seasoning, ½ teaspoon ground sage and ½ teaspoon ground thyme. In a large bowl, combine the onion mixture with 4 cups bread cubes and 1 cup chicken broth. Mix well. Place in a greased casserole and bake covered at 375° for 20 minutes. Remove the cover and bake another 5 minutes or until lightly browned. Or use as stuffing for poultry and bake as usual. **Yield:** 4 servings

John Shields'
Shrimp with OLD BAY Creole

John Shields, cookbook author and culinary ambassador of Chesapeake Bay cuisine, shared this bold creole with us— it's absolutely heady with flavor.

½ cup butter
1 cup finely chopped onion
1 green bell pepper, finely chopped
1 cup finely chopped celery
¼ cup all-purpose flour
4 cups peeled, coarsely chopped tomatoes
2 teaspoons OLD BAY Seasoning
½ teaspoon black pepper
2 tablespoons brown sugar
3 bay leaves
6 whole garlic cloves
1½ pounds raw medium shrimp, peeled and deveined
1 teaspoon Worcestershire sauce
Juice of ½ lemon
½ teaspoon hot sauce
Cooked white rice, as an accompaniment

In a heavy-bottomed pot, melt the butter and sauté the onion, green bell pepper and celery until soft. Stir in the flour and cook, stirring constantly, for 2 to 3 minutes.

Add the tomatoes, OLD BAY Seasoning, black pepper, brown sugar, bay leaves and garlic.

Bring to a boil. Reduce heat and simmer for about 1 hour. Stir often so the tomatoes do not stick to the bottom of the pot.

Add the shrimp, Worcestershire sauce, lemon juice and hot sauce and cook for about 20 minutes, or until shrimp are done. Serve over cooked white rice.

Yield: 6 servings

Perla Meyers'
Middle Eastern Char-Grilled Skirt Steaks

This marinated and grilled skirt steak created by Perla Meyers would be the perfect main course for a summer party.

Marinade:

¾ cup cumin seeds, lightly toasted
4 large garlic cloves, peeled
2 jalapeño peppers, cut in half
2 tablespoons cracked black pepper
2 canned chipotle peppers in adobo sauce
1 teaspoon OLD BAY Seasoning
6 bunches fresh cilantro, washed thoroughly and dried
1 to 1½ cups olive oil
Coarse salt, to taste

3 pounds skirt steak, trimmed of all excess fat
½ cup fresh lime juice
Sprigs of fresh cilantro, as a garnish

In a blender, process the cumin seeds until finely crushed. Add the garlic, jalapeño peppers, black pepper, chipotle peppers, OLD BAY Seasoning, cilantro and olive oil. Season highly with salt and process until smooth.

Cut the skirt steak into 6 pieces (about ½ pound each) and place them in a large resealable plastic bag. Pour the marinade over them and seal the bag. Set the bag in a shallow dish and refrigerate for 24 hours, turning the steaks in the marinade several times. Four hours before grilling, add the lime juice to the bag.

Prepare the charcoal grill. Remove the steaks from the bag and wipe off the excess marinade. When the coals are red-hot, sprinkle each side of the skirt steaks with a little coarse salt. Brush the grill with vegetable oil and place the steaks over the hot coals. Grill 2 to 3 minutes per side until nicely browned for medium rare, about 130 to 135° internal temperature on a meat thermometer.

Transfer the steaks to a cutting board and let sit for 2 to 3 minutes before slicing. Cut the meat across the grain into thin slices. Garnish with sprigs of cilantro.

Yield: 6 servings

OLD BAY TIP OF THE DAY

Spicy Marinade: In a self-closing plastic bag, combine ¼ cup vegetable oil, 2 tablespoons cider vinegar, 2 teaspoons OLD BAY seasoning, 1 teaspoon parsley flakes and ¼ teaspoon black pepper. Add 1 pound poultry or meat and marinate for 30 minutes in the refrigerator. Grill or broil. Yield: ⅓ cup marinade

Ilene Spector's
Green Bean and Potato Salad

Created by Ilene Spector, the syndicated food columnist, this is a terrific light summer variety of the traditional potato salad.

3 pounds cubed red skinned potatoes
½ pound fresh green beans, trimmed
½ cup chopped celery
½ cup chopped onion
¼ cup vegetable oil
1 tablespoon white wine vinegar
2 teaspoons OLD BAY Seasoning

Boil the potatoes in water for 6 minutes. Add the green beans. Boil 2 more minutes. Drain and rinse with cold water. Drain again.

In a large bowl, combine the potatoes and beans with the celery and onion. In a small bowl, combine the remaining ingredients. Toss with vegetables.

Chill 4 hours or more, stirring occasionally.

Yield: 6 to 8 servings

OLD BAY TIP OF THE DAY

Zesty Scrambled Eggs: Combine ¼ teaspoon or more OLD BAY Seasoning, 2 beaten eggs and 1 teaspoon water. In a small skillet over medium heat, melt 1 tablespoon butter. Pour the eggs into the hot butter and cook until scrambled. Yield: 1 serving

Fran Chapman's
Skillet Sizzle Cajun Fish

Fran Chapman, author of **Table for Two**, developed this recipe for one of the classes she teaches at L'Academie de Cuisine in Bethesda, MD. Fran owns Franch Enterprises, a business that includes recipe development for food manufacturers, culinary teaching and food marketing.

½ cup all-purpose flour
1 teaspoon ground thyme
1 teaspoon OLD BAY Seasoning
½ teaspoon salt
1 teaspoon paprika
¼ teaspoon red cayenne pepper, or to taste
Pinch of cloves
2 fillets firm fish, skinned and deboned
Canola oil, to oil skillet
4 tablespoons butter
Juice of ½ lemon

Combine the flour and seasonings in a small bowl. Set aside. Wash the fish and pat dry. Hold in refrigerator.

Oil a heavy cast-iron skillet with canola oil. Place the skillet in a cold oven, then set the temperature to 500°.

Melt the butter and add the lemon juice. Dip the fillets in the lemon butter mixture. Coat the fish with the flour mixture on both sides. Hold the remaining lemon butter.

After the oven temperature reaches 500°, remove the skillet from the oven and arrange the fillets in the hot skillet. Pour the remaining lemon butter mixture on top of the fish.

Bake 12 minutes in the oven. (Do not turn and do not open the oven door.)

Serve with a potato dish and a vegetable of choice.

Yield: 2 servings

Polly Clingerman's
Bayou Spiced Shrimp

These sassy shrimps come from Polly Clingerman, author of **The Kitchen Companion** and **Polly Clingerman's Dinner Companion**. The shrimp cook in a gloriously pungent oil loaded with spice and as much hot pepper as you dare to add. Provide plenty of napkins—this is a dish you eat with the fingers and with gusto!

2 slices bacon, in 1-inch pieces
⅔ cup vegetable oil
4 teaspoons OLD BAY Seasoning
1½ teaspoons chili powder
¾ teaspoon mixed Italian herbs
4 teaspoons Dijon mustard
2 cloves garlic, minced
Hot pepper sauce, to taste
1 pound large shrimp in their shells
Cooked white rice

Preheat the oven to 375°.

In a medium ovenproof skillet, fry the bacon over medium heat until soft. Add the vegetable oil. Reduce heat to low and add the OLD BAY Seasoning, chili powder, Italian herbs, Dijon mustard and garlic cloves. Let the mixture bubble for about 1 minute. Add the hot pepper sauce to taste (anywhere from ¼ to ½ teaspoon).

Put the unshelled shrimp in the seasoned oil and stir them around until completely coated. Place the skillet in the oven and bake uncovered for 20 minutes.

Serve the shrimp with steamed rice and French bread.

Yield: 4 servings

OLD BAY Classics

Who would have known more than 50 years ago that OLD BAY® Seasoning would have such an impact on Chesapeake Bay cooking? Today, Marylanders wouldn't dream of steaming crabs, preparing shrimp or making the robust tomato-based Maryland crab soup without this bold spice.

Yet cooks are beginning to find that OLD BAY's blend of herbs and spices brings to life simple dining pleasures. Replacing salt and pepper as the region's favorite condiment, OLD BAY adds zest to everything from fries and popcorn to even pizza. We invite you to use OLD BAY to make an easy summer marinade for chicken. Or add a teaspoon to mayonnaise for extra flavor on your favorite chicken or fish sandwich.

Relish the taste of these classic and easy-to-prepare recipes. They're a collection of simple ideas with abundant flavor that celebrate the Chesapeake Bay dining experience.

Hot Artichoke and Crab Dip

This is a delicious answer to the question of what to serve when guests drop in for a visit.

½ cup mayonnaise
½ cup sour cream
1 can (7 ounces) artichoke hearts, chopped and drained
6½ ounces fresh lump crabmeat
⅓ cup grated fresh Parmesan cheese
⅛ teaspoon hot sauce
½ teaspoon OLD BAY Seasoning

Mix all ingredients and place in a small casserole dish.
Bake at 350° for about 20 minutes, or until hot and bubbly.
Serve with assorted crackers.
Yield: about 2 cups

OLD BAY TIP OF THE DAY

Party Dip: Combine 1 pint sour cream, 1 cup mayonnaise, 3 tablespoons sliced green onions and 1 teaspoon OLD BAY Seasoning. Cover and refrigerate 1 hour or more. Serve with cut-up fresh vegetables and potato chips. **Yield:** *3 cups dip*

Layered Seafood Appetizer

Impress guests with this pretty appetizer. Serve with assorted crackers or plain tortilla chips. Sprinkle with additional OLD BAY Seasoning just before serving.

2 packages (8 ounces each) cream cheese, softened
2 tablespoons mayonnaise
1 tablespoon OLD BAY Seasoning
½ cup sliced green onion, green part only
¾ cup diced tomato
1 pound lump crabmeat
½ cup shredded Cheddar cheese

In a medium bowl, cream together the cream cheese, mayonnaise and OLD BAY Seasoning. Evenly spread in the bottom of a pizza pan or a 12-inch round tray. Sprinkle the onion and the tomato over the cream cheese mixture. Top with the crabmeat and Cheddar cheese. Sprinkle with additional OLD BAY Seasoning, if desired.

Yield: about 10 servings

OLD BAY TIP OF THE DAY

Vegetables in Foil: Sprinkle 1 teaspoon OLD BAY Seasoning over 4 cups sliced or chopped vegetables such as onions, squash, mushrooms, potatoes or tomatoes. Wrap in heavy aluminum foil and grill or broil until done.

Steamed Shrimp

A seafood classic, Marylanders wouldn't dream of cooking shrimp any other way. This spicy, distinctive-flavored shrimp is great as a party appetizer.

½ cup vinegar
½ cup water
1 tablespoon OLD BAY Seasoning
1 teaspoon salt
1 pound shrimp, shells on

Cocktail Sauce:

1 cup ketchup
1½ teaspoons OLD BAY Seasoning
½ teaspoon prepared horseradish

In saucepan, combine the vinegar, water, OLD BAY Seasoning and salt. Bring to a boil. Add the shrimp and stir gently.

Cover and steam until tender, about 5 minutes.

To make the cocktail sauce: Combine the ketchup, OLD BAY Seasoning and horseradish. Chill before serving.

Yield: 3 to 4 servings

OLD BAY TIP OF THE DAY

*Tomato Juice Cocktail: Combine 1 can (24 ounces) chilled tomato juice with 1½ teaspoons **OLD BAY** Seasoning. Pour into glasses and garnish with celery stalks. **Yield:** 4 servings*

Fresh Shrimp Salad

Serve on croissants, sandwich rolls or a bed of leaf lettuce.

1 pound fresh medium shrimp, cooked, peeled and deveined
½ cup mayonnaise
⅔ cup chopped celery
2 teaspoons OLD BAY Seasoning
2 teaspoons fresh lemon juice
¼ teaspoon Worcestershire sauce

Cut shrimp in half.

Combine shrimp, mayonnaise, celery, OLD BAY Seasoning, lemon juice and Worcestershire sauce.

Cover the shrimp salad and refrigerate 30 minutes or more. Stir before serving.

Yield: 4 servings

OLD BAY TIP OF THE DAY

Seasoned Mayonnaise: Blend ½ *teaspoon or more* **OLD BAY** *Seasoning into ½ cup mayonnaise. Spread on hamburgers, crab cakes or fish sandwiches.* **Yield:** *½ cup*

Spicy Marinade

This marinade is delicious for grilling chicken breasts, steaks or shish kebab.

¼ cup vegetable oil
2 tablespoons cider vinegar
2 teaspoons OLD BAY Seasoning
1 teaspoon dried parsley
¼ teaspoon ground black pepper
1 pound chicken breasts or beefsteaks

In a self-closing plastic bag, combine the vegetable oil, cider vinegar, OLD BAY Seasoning, parsley and black pepper.

Add the chicken breasts or beefsteaks and marinate 30 minutes.

Grill or broil the chicken or beef until done.

Yield: ⅓ cup marinade

OLD BAY TIP OF THE DAY

Flavor Enhancer: Wake up the flavor of favorite foods—try sprinkling a little *OLD BAY* Seasoning on pizza, popcorn and pasta.

Seasoned Vegetable Spread

Try this seasoned butter on corn on the cob, bread, grilled fish or vegetables.

½ cup butter, softened
2 teaspoons fresh lemon juice
1½ teaspoons OLD BAY Seasoning
½ teaspoon instant minced onion

In a small bowl, whip the butter until very soft. Add the lemon juice, OLD BAY Seasoning and minced onion.
Yield: about ½ cup

OLD BAY TIP OF THE DAY

Flavorful French Fries: Cook fresh or frozen fries. Sprinkle with 1 to 2 teaspoons OLD BAY Seasoning before serving.

OLD BAY Shrimp Crisps

This is a low-fat recipe, so serve it when guests are watching their waistlines.

1½ cups water
1½ teaspoons OLD BAY Seasoning, divided
¾ pound medium shrimp, peeled and deveined
2 tablespoons finely chopped green onion
2 tablespoons finely chopped red bell pepper
1 tablespoon chopped fresh parsley
2 tablespoons water
1 teaspoon olive oil
1 egg white
6 thin slices whole wheat bread, lightly toasted
Reduced-fat mayonnaise

In a saucepan, combine 1½ cups water and ½ teaspoon OLD BAY Seasoning. Bring the water to a boil. Add the shrimp and cook 3 to 5 minutes or until the shrimp turn pink. Drain well and let cool.

Finely chop the shrimp. Place in a medium bowl. Add the green onions, 1 teaspoon OLD BAY Seasoning, red bell pepper, parsley, water, olive oil and egg white. Stir until well blended.

Trim the crusts from the bread slices. Spread lightly with reduced-fat mayonnaise.

Spoon the shrimp mixture evenly over the bread slices. Cut each slice of bread into 4 triangles. Place the triangles on a large baking sheet coated with cooking spray.

Bake at 350° for 8 to 10 minutes or until thoroughly heated and lightly browned.

Yield: about 24 crisps

Seasoned Fried Chicken

This fried chicken has just the right flavor. If desired, sprinkle the cooked chicken with additional OLD BAY seasoning right before serving.

1 cup all-purpose flour
¼ cup OLD BAY Seasoning
1 egg, beaten
2 tablespoons water
2 cups vegetable oil
2 to 3 pounds chicken parts

In a large plastic bag, combine the flour and OLD BAY Seasoning. In a shallow dish, combine the egg and water.

Place the vegetable oil in a large skillet over medium-high heat, to a depth of at least 2 inches. Heat to 365°.

Dip the chicken into the egg mixture, then place a few pieces of chicken at a time into the plastic bag. Shake until the chicken is well coated.

Place chicken into the hot oil in a single layer and cook about 20 minutes per side, or until done.

Drain the cooked chicken on paper towels to remove some excess oil before serving.

Yield: 6 to 8 servings

OLD BAY TIP OF THE DAY

Spicy Hamburgers: Using your hands or a wooden spoon, mix 2 teaspoons OLD BAY Seasoning into a pound of ground beef. Shape into four patties and grill the burgers to desired doneness. Serve on buns with cheese, ketchup, mustard, pickles or other toppings. **Yield:** *4 hamburgers*

Maryland Crab Soup

There is nothing nicer than a pot of Maryland Crab Soup simmering on the stove on a chilly day. Serve it as a first course or for the main course with salad and bread as accompaniments.

3 cans (10¼ ounces each) beef broth
6 cups water
¼ cup chopped onion
2 tablespoons OLD BAY Seasoning
2 cans (16 ounces each) diced or whole tomatoes, undrained
2 packages (10 ounces each) frozen mixed vegetables
5 cups potatoes, coarsely chopped
1 pound fresh crabmeat, all shell removed

In a large soup pot, combine the beef broth, water, onion and OLD BAY Seasoning. Bring to a boil.

Add the tomatoes, mixed vegetables and potatoes. Simmer 1½ hours.

Stir in the crabmeat. Simmer for another hour.

Yield: 10 to 12 servings

OLD BAY TIP OF THE DAY

Flavorful Tuna Salad: Combine 1 can drained tuna, ½ cup mayonnaise, 1 tablespoon chopped onion, 1 tablespoon chopped celery and ¾ teaspoon OLD BAY Seasoning. Add extra mayonnaise or OLD BAY Seasoning to taste. **Yield:** *2 servings*

Index

Order Toll Free! 1-800-8-OLD BAY

Or write to: OLD BAY Bounty From The Bay
P.O. Box 15062, St. Louis, MO 63110

100% Cotton Hanes BeefyT-Shirt
Show our good taste with this thick, heavy and oversized, 100% preshrunk cotton t-shirt with a giant OLD BAY can logo on the back. *White. Sizes: M, L, XL*   **T-shirt $12.99**

OLD BAY Soup Mug
This weighty ceramic soup mug is as hearty as your homemade soups and chowders.
16-ounce soup mugs   **Set of 4 mugs $34.99 One mug $8.99**

OLD BAY Shakers
Bring OLD BAY® out of the cupboard! Choose a pewter OLD BAY shaker, or a Pfaltzgraff® ceramic round shaker with a handle. **Ceramic shaker $12.99**   **Pewter shaker $19.99**

DishTowel and Pot Holder Set
Show your good taste with a durable, heavyweight white cotton dish towel and royal blue 8" quilted pot holder. Both feature the OLD BAY logo.   **Dish Towel & Pot Holder Set $12.99**

Chef's Apron
Durable, heavyweight 100% cotton apron with roomy pockets and adjustable neck straps and ties.
Royal blue with color logo.   **29" x 34" Apron $19.99**

QTY	ITEM	SIZE	PRICE EA.	TOTAL

Merchandise Total	
Sales Tax (MO only)	
Shipping & Handling	
Rush Delivery	
TOTAL AMOUNT DUE	

SHIPPING & HANDLING
(per delivery address)

Merchandise total:	Add:
Up to $5.00	$4.50
$5.01 to $10.00	$5.50
$10.01 to $20.00	$6.25
$20.01 to $30.00	$7.00
$30.01 to $40.00	$7.75
$40.01 to $80.00	$8.50
$80.00 and over—add 10% of merchandise total	

RUSH DELIVERY:

UPS Next Day Delivery
            Add $14.95 additional
UPS 2nd Day Delivery
            Add $8.95 additional

Please allow 3 to 4 weeks for delivery.

Offer good in the Continental US only, while supplies last.

SOLDTO:
For gifts, write names & addresses on separate paper. No PO boxes please)

Name_____

Addres_____

City _____ State _____

Zip _____ Daytime Phone _____

PAYMENT METHOD:
❑ **Check/money order** (Payable to: OLD BAY Bounty From The Bay)
❑ **VISA**   ❑ **Mastercard**   ❑ **Discover**

Account Number _____

Expiration Date _____

Cardholder Signature _____